Teaching Students

Thinking
Skills

By: Monica Sevilla

Contents

1. Teaching Our Students How To Think

We know as educators, through extensive research, that if we ask our students to use the higher thinking levels of Bloom's taxonomy, it builds their critical thinking and problem solving skills. Educators at every level complain that our students can not "think". What does this mean?. The most fundamental complaint of employers is that students leaving the colleges and entering the workforce have difficulty "applying the knowledge they have learned to new problems and situations, They struggle with logically thinking through and solving problems". What this essentially means to educators is that our students are weak or have not sufficiently developed the skills associated at the higher levels of Bloom's taxonomy (i.e. at the applying, analyzing, evaluating, and creating stages. The "basic" critical thinking and problem solving skills needed for entry level employment need to be strengthened. What are we doing as educators to remedy this?

The traditional school system spends too much time on instruction aimed at the the lower levels of Bloom's taxonomy, namely the "remembering" and "understanding" levels and not enough time at the higher levels. If we as educators are not progressing past these two stages, we are doing our students a disservice and setting them up for failure in the future. We can only blame ourselves for not teaching them how to think, not presenting them enough opportunities or practice to develop these skills. If this is our reality, then we need to rethink our priorities. The manner in which we instruct our students needs to change. Redesigning our curriculums to incorporate and accommodate the learning of the skills at the higher levels of Bloom's taxonomy will take precedent in order to facilitate the development of these skills and ensure that our students do learn how to "think" in the truest sense of the word.

2. Bloom's Taxonomy: A Process of Thinking

How Do We Learn? We learn by constructing knowledge through following distinct "levels" of thinking described in Bloom's Taxonomy. The following is the new representation of Bloom's taxonomy:

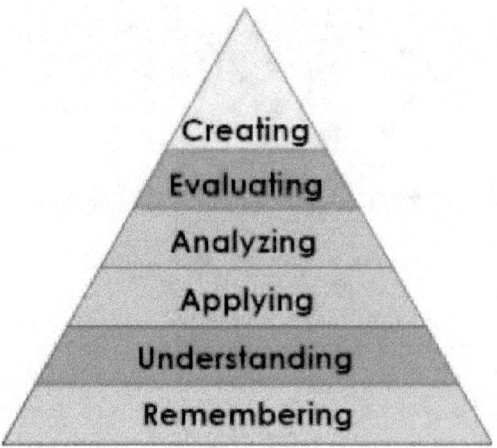

In 1956, Benjamin Bloom and a team of educational psychologists developed a classification or taxonomy of levels of cognitive skills for the development of thinking and learning. In the 1990's, a new group lead by Lorin Anderson (a former student of Bloom's. The group updated the taxonomy in reflection of work done 21st century . This is a new representation of Bloom's Taxonomy. Nouns have been changed to action words (Verbs) to describe the different levels. Action words more accurately depict the "active" nature of the process of learning.

Oliver Wendell Holmes and Art Costa described it as:

"Before we can **understand** a concept we have to **remember** it

Before we can **apply** the concept we must **understand** it

Before we **analyze** it we must be able to **apply** it

Before we can **evaluate** its impact we must have **analyzed** it

Before we can **create** we must have **remembered, understood, applied, analyzed,** and **evaluated**."

This description outlines the process or pattern of thinking students follow to construct a meaningful framework for learning knowledge and skills. Certain learning objectives and tasks must be accomplished before others. Learning can start at any level in this process. Each level becomes "cumulative" of the knowledge and skills in the levels preceding it. Basic knowledge and skills are acquired at the "knowledge" and "understanding" levels of Bloom's taxonomy. This is where the foundation of learning is created.

Remembering:

Remembering knowledge and skills at the basic level of Bloom's taxonomy can be done by daily practice and its incorporation into the understanding of knowledge and skills in the next level and built into the routine. Activities can be in the form of memory aids, concept maps, and graphic organizers.These activities could be done the first 5-10 minutes in class as a warm-up or the last 5-10 minutes of class as a review or recap of what was learned that day. Remembering knowledge is the responsibility of the student to also practice at home.

examples:

define, duplicate, list, memorize, recall, repeat, reproduce, state

Understanding:

Students must understand key concepts and skills before they are expected to apply and use it in novel situations. This is the expectation that society places on learners throughout their lives in the workplace. Students must be able to understand what they've learned and clearly communicate it to others.

Activities geared to the understanding and comprehension of key concepts in a unit of study should be carefully planned out and should directly support the main topic. Students should also be asked to demonstrate their understanding through a written assignment such as summarizing, describing, and identifying and in-class discussion, reporting out, and explaining so they gain the practice and experience in written communication and verbal expression.

Examples: classify, describe, discuss, explain, identify, locate, recognize, report, select, translate, paraphrase.

Applying:

Students, when they enter the workplace, must be able to take the knowledge they have learned and apply it in new ways. At this level, practice and opportunities to gain this practice becomes critical. An ample amount of time must be invested at this stage to ensure that the student develops these skills properly. The consequence of not doing so becomes devastating. Here is where the students first learn critical thinking and problem solving skills. The burden is placed squarely on the teacher to introduce strategies, tasks, and activities to develop and strengthen these skills. Best practices include giving students reflection questions they can answer and record in a notebook.

Questions can be related to cause and effect, extrapolate thinking, make predictions based on what you know, explain possible outcomes, and demonstrate your thinking. Questions should stimulate thinking and provoke thought.

Examples: choose, demonstrate, dramatize, employ, illustrate, interpret, operate, schedule, sketch, solve, use, **write**.

It is interesting to note that writing is listed as an example of a skill at the "applying" level. Let's examine why this is. Writing at this level not only incorporate the physical action of writing but also the metacognitive skill of writing. We are essential asking our students to recall what they have learned, explain what they know, apply this knowledge to new, novel situations or in a new format in written form. They are essentially using the information they have learned and communicating their thoughts and ideas to others. This is one of the main expectations society has deemed as an essential skill for hiring and promotion in the workforce. Students who are weak in this area encounter one of the harsh realities of life. The diminished availability of career options and opportunities.

If we are to sufficiently prepare our students for the future, we must first teach this skill with fidelity, and offer many opportunities to our students for the practice and development of this skill. Neglect and avoidance on our part will directly impact the future of our students. The consequences of our actions will result in our students inability to be hired or promoted by existing businesses for lack of the entry level skills needed to become successful employees. Their failure is our failure!

Analyzing:

Students analyze or examine data, observations, and information they have, sort it into distinct categories to differentiate between them, and also recognize patterns that emerge. Students at this level are able to "see" the similarities and differences, and differentiate between types of data and observations. Students can then make informed decisions, judgments, and conclusions from it.

Examples: appraise, compare, contrast, criticize, differentiate, discriminate, distinguish, examine, experiment, **question**, test.

Evaluating:

Students take the information and evidence they have analyzed, and make informed decisions, judgments, and conclusions from it. The student is able to defend, support, or make a judgment about a claim or position based on the data they have seen.

examples: appraise, **argue**, **defend**, judge, select, **support**, value, evaluate.

Creating:

The level of "Creating" within the learning process incorporates all the levels preceding it. The most effective learning projects for students are ones which they create, design, plan, and write themselves to demonstrate their mastery of key concepts and skills .

The fundamental critical thinking and problem solving skills students need to master are found in the "applying", "analyzing", and "evaluating" levels of Bloom's taxonomy. Once mastered, these skills ultimately work together in synergy and also complement one another in the "**Creating**" level of Bloom's taxonomy. It is at this level that students get the "most bang for their buck."

Most of the academic gains in standardized testing are the outcome of projects created by students at this level. These projects incorporate the the problem solving and critical thinking skills found in the "applying", "analyzing", and "evaluating" levels of Bloom's Taxonomy along with understanding and comprehending the basic knowledge and skills in the "remembering" and "understanding" levels. Projects created at this level are well rounded, well planned, incorporate a dynamic range of tasks and assignments that students can see how they inter-connect and all play an important role in the "big picture".

Thinking skills associated with the "Creating" level of Bloom's taxonomy:

assemble, construct, create, design, develop, formulate, write, plan, produce, invent, devise, make.

Projects incorporating the following skills demonstrate learning at the highest level of Bloom's taxonomy, the "Creating" level:

Publishing (eBooks, eNotebooks, eMagazines, reports, ePortfolios, eJournals, articles, wikis, blogs, tweets, plans), animating, filming (making movies), videocasting, podcasting, creating multimedia presentations, and broadcasting.

3. Inquiry Learning and Asking Meaningful Questions

Inquiry Learning is a type of learning that allows students to construct new knowledge while seeking information through asking questions. One of the most useful outcomes of inquiry learning is that it constructs knowledge that can be applied to a wide range of new situations. Asking a question is the driving force of discovery. All scientific studies start by asking a question, making a prediction or a "guess" to what we think the answer is, and finding evidence to support or refute our predictions, and provide answer that question. We all gather information and make observations about the world around us through our sense of sight, hearing, smell, taste, and touch. These observations are the "evidence" or the "proof" to make a sound conclusion in regard to our predictions.

Giving students more opportunities to ask questions through inquiry projects allow students more practice and time to develop critical thinking and problem solving skills. Students must be encouraged to ask their own questions, learn by seeking their own evidence, and answer their own questions. We must minimize the "hand-feeding" of knowledge through passive means of instruction, and allow students to become fully engaged in project learning within our classes. We must become the facilitators of their own learning instead of the teacher who lectures everyday at the head of the class. If we are to encourage our students to be independent thinkers, we should put them in the driver's seat and in charge of their own learning.

Teachers must ask meaningful and relevant questions designed to allow students to use and practice critical thinking and problem solving skills.

Encourage students to respond to these questions, in an interactive notebook as a "reflection" and citing evidence to support their claims. Their written response becomes the evidence of what they are "thinking" and assesses where they are in their understanding and application of the knowledge and skills they have learned. Allow them to discuss their responses with you and other students in the class. By doing so, students will receive critical feedback from their peers and also learn by listening to other perspectives and explanations.

4. Interactive Notebooks

Interactive notebooks are an effective strategy for students to record notes and reflect on what they have written. Research shows that students need to revisit concepts 7 or more times in order to commit them to their long term memories. Students are able to construct knowledge by processing these concepts through their own interpretation and writing.

Allows students to record their notes, data, and evidence presented in class in one part of the notebook and "interact" with this information by writing reflections in the other. (on opposing pages of their notebook). Students, ideally, are engaged in activities and are asked to record what they are doing on the right-hand pages. On the left-hand page, they are asked to "think about their own thinking" and write   their thoughts, opinions, feelings, and epiphanies.

Left Page reflections	Right Page notes, data, evidence
Construct knowledge by reorganizing information in new ways	class notes: text, pictures, concept maps, graphic organizers new knowledge and skills
express opinions, feelings	discussion notes
explore new ideas	reading notes
questions and responses to questions	handouts with new information
responses to readings	data tables, observations, photos, etc (for science and lab experiments)

The example below demonstrates how teachers can use Interactive notebooks within their classes. This example, reading and writing about an article, can be used across the curriculum, in almost any subject area:

Left Page reflections	Right Page notes, data, evidence
Students can write: * a summary of the article itself. * thoughts and feelings about the article * draw pictures related to the article. * ask questions about the article. * write down 5-10 important key words mentioned in the article *responses to discussion questions given by the teacher	notes taken on an article related to a topic or unit of study. A student is reading this article in class as an activity.

There are many reasons why Interactive notebooks are an effective tool for learning. Some of the benefits of using them include:

• Assists in the development of language development and writing

• encourages them to think independently

• Learn to improve organization

• allows them to brainstorm

• make information their own and interact with this information

• allows students to be creative

• skills of metacognition...they think about their own thinking through reflection

• becomes an archive of information they can review for assessments and use in the completion of projects

- creates high intrinsic motivation

- can be incorporated into any subject

- Notes can include "" or "evidence" of learning: text, pictures, graphic organizers, concept maps,

- Can be use as an authentic assessment of student learning...assess they're understanding of concepts and determine whether they have mastered it

5. Writing Across the Curriculum

Writing is an activity and form of communication that expresses thought in a written form. It is an essential entry-level employment skill that businesses today use to determine the hiring and promoting of employees. Employers require reports to be written and paperwork to be completed as part of their job requirements. Our students must possess and master this skill to ensure them the opportunity and availability of a career in the future.

The purpose of writing is:

* to communicate information
* to clarify thinking (working through an idea or problem in writing)
* to construct knowledge and to learn new concepts (taking notes, responding to literature, researching topics)

Students must develop the skill of writing as a daily practice. Research shows that students need to learn and master the art of writing at an early age and frequently in order to be college and career ready. By incorporating relevant and meaningful writing assignments into the curriculum, we can develop and strengthen our students' writing and communication skills.

Writing assignments do not have to be long or complex. They just need to be authentic and meaningful to the students and within the subject area at hand. Assignments and activities must peak the interests of our students and engage them in thinking.

6. Creating Writing Projects that Incorporate Thinking Skills

Writing assignments should also be designed at the higher levels of Bloom's taxonomy such as "creating", "evaluating, and "analyzing." This will ensure they are writing at a high enough level to practice and develop critical thinking and problem-solving skills on a daily basis. Some useful and practical examples include:

• Using Interactive notebooks

• Using daily eJournals (or a diary) to write your thoughts and feelings of about different issues in your life

• Responses to literature and articles

• Responses to thought-provoking questions

• Responses or feedback to the comments of others

• Classroom Blogs

• writing a summary about a reading, a video clip, or what someone has said

• State your position about an issue or current event and support your position with 3 pieces of evidence

• Constructing Venn diagrams

- Constructing Pros vs. Cons Chart on an issue and make a judgment based on the data

- Make predictions and conclusions based on data and evidence

Writing is most powerful when it occurs across the curriculum. Projects and assignments designed to inter-connect ideas from different disciplines have been shown to result in a high retention rate of information. Not only do students remember the concepts longer, they also show increased gains on standardized testing. The most effective projects are those created by the students. Examples of such projects can be in the form of research reports formatted as eBooks, multimedia presentations, podcasts, vodcasts, and iMovies.

7. Effective Projects for Assessing Thinking Skills

Creating projects is the most effective assessment of learning concepts and skills. Research shows that students who are able to demonstrate their learning in projects developed at the "Creating" level of Bloom's Taxonomy are able to retain the information longer and score higher on the standardized tests. In leu of having students show that they mastered knowledge and skills on a paper-based exam or cumulative final, research or inquiry projects can be used instead. These projects are a more authentic way of assessing the skills of remembering, understanding, applying, analyzing, and evaluating key concepts and skills for a unit or period of study.

The beauty of this type of assignment is that they incorporate the problem solving and critical thinking skills found in the "applying", "analyzing", and "evaluating" levels of Bloom's Taxonomy along with understanding and comprehending the basic knowledge and skills in the "remembering" and "understanding" levels. Projects created at this level are well rounded, well planned, incorporate a dynamic range of tasks and assignments that students can see how they inter-connect together to form the "big picture" in the minds of our students. Excellent examples of projects that can be given to students at the "creating" level include: Publishing (eBooks, interactive eNotebooks, eMagazines, ePortfolios, eJournals, articles, iMovies, videocasting, podcasting, creating multimedia presentations such as Powerpoint and Keynote, and broadcasting.

8. eBooks as Examples of Projects Demonstrating Thinking Skills

The eBook is a wonderful way to publish your written works quickly and conveniently. They can be available to the public with the click of a button. The eBook is merely a written book available in electronic or digital format. Many publishers now offer books in print as well as in electronic or digital form. The eBook is created and written in a word processing

application, converted to a PDF or an EPub file, uploaded onto an online publisher's website, and sold to prospective readers. Many books in print have been digitalized and posted online as eBooks.

Many professions now exist online through the use of the Internet that didn't 20 years ago. One such profession is ePublishing or writing and publishing books in electronic or digital format. writing articles for websites, blogs, and eBooks. With the convenience of internet access and online publishers, anyone could write and publish in their pajamas and submit their written works to their employers and publishers from home.

The good news here is that students (as well as adults) could learn relevant ePublishing skills, namely writing, communication tools, and web skills within minutes, and be able to use them fluidly. It is not limited to age. For students, the skills and guidelines they would need for ePublishing profession in the future, can be easily be taught through assignments, activities, and projects they do in their content areas. These assignments and activities can be developed to simulate what they would encounter in the workplace such as a career in ePublishing. Preparing our students with 21 st century skills is of the upmost importance. The more real life experiences and opportunities they are given in the classroom now, the more successful they will be in the real world in the future. Students will be able to directly translate their ePublishing skills to jobs requiring specific skills in computer technology and writing.   Ask yourself this vital question:

How many jobs in the future will require the knowledge and training computer technology skills?

There are many practical uses for eBooks in the field of Education. eBooks are powerful tools that teachers can create for the instruction of core content knowledge to be accessed by the student. eBooks created by the students help them demonstrate their mastery of content skills and also strengthen their verbal and written communication skills. The practical uses of eBooks are many. One important use of eBooks is its ability to engage students in the skill and the art of writing.   The more writing opportunities teachers make available to their students, the more practice they will get, and the more confident they will become.

Teachers can create eBook unit lessons or eLessons as PDFs and post them on their websites for students to download. eBook lessons may contain the unit lesson, images, vocabulary terms to know, assignments, and assessments. eBook documents created in Word, Pages, Powerpoint and Keynote all suffice and can be converted to PDF files. The practical uses of eLessons is that students can access the content within the lesson and learn at their own pace. They are also able to access this information 24/7, from home, and during the summer. Learning can take place anytime, anywhere. eBooks serve as a product of student learning and mastery of subject area content that can be monitored and assessed. eBooks allow students to demonstrate content knowledge and skills learned over a specified period of time. eBooks can be used in leu of the traditional paper-based project. Book reports, science fair reports, content area reports, and cross-curricular reports requiring web-based research can naturally be created and saved as an eBook. It's a great way to "go green", save a few trees, and create a product that can be saved in digital format.

9. How To Create A Simple eBook

Choose the topic the students will focus in their eBook. Be certain to add the ELA goals for reading, writing, and communication for their grade level. Decide what criteria the students will meet and what they will write about in their eBook project to demonstrate their mastery of the content knowledge and skills for the topic they are presently learning! This can be done by having students write about and research the major learning objectives for the topic they are learning.

• Develop a rubric for grading your students eBook project.

• Choose a computer software that is easy to manage and that offers many writing, editing, and graphic tools such as Word, Pages, Powerpoint or Keynote.   The writing process does not need to be complicated by using software that will cause a lot of grief and headaches in the long run.

• Write a brief set of instructions, based on the criteria you have developed for the eBook for your students.

• Walk them through the major features of the application your students will be using.

• Go through the eProject instructions you have written with your students step by step.

• Have your students create the cover, title page, and content page for their eBook.

- Next have them save their work. Have your students write the major sections (chapters) including text pages and picture pages for their book according to the criteria you set in their instructions.

- Have your students select pictures from searching in Google images and have them drag & drop them into their book project.

- When they are finished with their eBook, have them save their work as a PDF. These documents can be easily be converted to a PDF and saved by going to the "File" menu of the application you are working with, clicking on print, and choosing the "Save as PDF button".

- Have your students save your PDF when they are finished with their project on your desktop, in separate folder, or on a thumb drive. Many documents can be saved in this standardized format, posted on websites or sent to others without the fuss!

For examples of written eBooks, visit:

https://sites.google.com/site/eclassroom4teachers/Home

eClassroom 4 Teachers

TRANSFORMING
the World of Education

The vision of the eClassroom 4 Teachers website is to help educators such as yourself, learn about the latest technology and how it can be integrated and applied as a powerful learning tool in the curriculum. eClassroom for Teachers was created and designed for educators to attain these technological skills. By integrating technology in the classroom, educators are able to teach their students how to use 21st century technological skills now and in the future.

Visit Our Website at:

https://sites.google.com/site/eclassroom4teachers/Home

www.ingramcontent.com/pod-product-compliance
Lightning Source LLC
Chambersburg PA
CBHW071328310526
45789CB00016B/1881